Mommy, Can You Teach Me How to Budget?

Written By
Annette Harris

Edited By
Dweise Harris

ISBN: 979-8-9884073-4-8

To Destiny & Dontavious,

Both of you have inspired me to grow and mature in life. Through life's major lessons, we have all learned how we can achieve great things and overcome challenges. I wish you both continued success.

Love,
Mom

Destiny and Trey, teenagers filled with ambition, took a break from playing their video game. Destiny notices Trey is in deep thought.

"Trey, what are you daydreaming about this time?" Destiny asked playfully.

"I am just thinking. We both have saved a lot of money from gifts, chores, and our jobs. I am just trying to figure out what I am going to spend it on. What do you plan to do with all the money you saved?" asked Trey.

"Since I started working at the grocery store after school, I've been spending my money on clothes, makeup, and pizza. What about you?" asked Destiny.

Trey thought for a minute and said, "You know what, I've been spending my money on clothes, video games, and music, but I've been trying to think of a better way to handle my money."

"Do you have any ideas?" asked Destiny.

"Not really. Maybe we should ask Mom. She always has great ideas about money," said Trey.

The aroma of freshly baked cookies filled the air as Destiny and Trey walked into their kitchen. They looked at each other and nodded in agreement about their plan.

"Hi, Mommy!" Destiny and Trey exclaimed.

"Hi, Destiny and Trey. What's up?" asked Mom.

"Mom, Destiny, and I have questions about the money we make from our jobs. Do you have a few minutes to talk about it?" asked Trey.

“Sure, I always have time to talk about money and your goals. So, what questions do you have?” asked Mom, setting down the tray of cookies.

“Mommy, I spend a lot of my money on clothes, makeup, and lots of pizza,” said Destiny.

“And I spend my money on clothes, video games, and music. But we both want to know if there’s a better way to manage our money,” said Trey.

Mom listens while Trey and Destiny continue to explain their thoughts.

"As you know, Mom, I'm getting older and want to be more independent. One of my goals on my vision board is to purchase a car soon," said Trey.

"And I want to be able to put some of my money away for college. Can you help us?" asked Destiny.

"Well, those are both very big goals you have, and it's going to take some time and planning for you to achieve them. But it's not impossible if you budget your money," said Mom, smiling.

"Let's go over to the kitchen table, and let me teach you how to budget. Grab your notebooks and something to write with," said Mom.

"Mommy, what is budgeting?" asked Destiny and Trey simultaneously.

"That's a great question. Budgeting helps you prioritize what you want and need to spend your money on in a certain period of time. When I budget monthly, I make sure all our bills, like our cell phones, car payments, electricity, and groceries, are paid first before spending money on other things.

For example, before we go to the movies, out to a restaurant, or on a vacation, I pay all our monthly bills first," said Mom.

Destiny reminded her mom of a previous lesson, "Remember when you taught me how to save money? You had me draw a picture of everything I wanted to buy and then write numbers next to them, starting with one, two, and three. This helped me prioritize what I wanted. You always say that having priorities is very important."

"That's right," her mom replied. "The concept is similar."

"What happens if you don't pay those bills first?" asked Trey.

"There could be late fees. That means I would have to pay extra for not paying the bill on time. It's sort of like a penalty in football. When there's a delay in the game, the team may lose five yards to make sure they play on time. Paying your bills on time is very similar to that. The bank or cell phone company wants to make sure we pay on time, and if we don't, then you have to pay extra money," explained Mom.

"Mommy, have you ever paid a bill late and had to pay a penalty?" asked Destiny.

"Yes, at least once that I can remember, but I immediately paid the bill and made sure that it wouldn't happen again. We all make money mistakes, but as long as you learn from them, it will stop you from making that same mistake again, and a budget helps," said Mom.

"Now, let's talk about budgeting and prioritizing your goals," said Mom.

"We'll go step by step in setting up a budget. First, you're going to want to write down the money that you earn from your job; that's your income. Take a look at your bank accounts and see what you were paid last month. Write down the last four paychecks you received," said Mom.

Destiny and Trey listed all their income in their notebooks.

After Destiny and Trey finished reviewing their income, Mom guided them to list their expenses.

Mom explained that there are two types of expenses: fixed and variable.

She reminded Destiny and Trey that fixed expenses were items like the mortgage, the cell phone bill, or their car payment. These expenses are essential and stay the same from month to month.

Variable expenses can change and are used for things like eating out, clothes, and financial goals, like saving for a car or college.

"You should both be honest and realistic about what you spend your money on," said Mom.

As they listed their expenses, Destiny, who loved clothes and eating out, had to face the reality of her spending habits. Trey also realized how much he spent on video games and decided that his car purchase would require stricter control over his spending.

Finally came the crucial step – budgeting. Mom guided them through the process of building their budget. This required Destiny and Trey to divide their income between their needs, wants, and goals. “Remember,” Mom emphasized, “the most important thing is prioritizing. You have to decide what’s truly important to you and budget your money accordingly.”

As the list grew, Mom introduced them to the 50/30/20 rule, explaining that 50% of their income should go towards needs, 30% towards wants, and 20% towards savings.

"This rule is a guideline, not a rigid rule," she explained. "You can adjust it based on your needs and goals.

Mom also introduced the concept of "pay yourself first." She explained to them that this is a budgeting strategy that encourages setting aside money for themselves before paying for other variable expenses.

"For example, if you receive $125 from your paycheck every week, you can automatically transfer $25 into your savings account for your future goals," Mom said.

"Oh! It's like the first bill you pay first is yourself," exclaimed Trey.

"Absolutely! You worked hard for that money, so you should reward yourself first," replied Mom with a smile.

Mom explained that this would help them avoid the temptation to spend money sitting in their checking accounts and keep them motivated.

Trey looked at his mom and said, "So, Mom, how much should we save for our goals?"

Mom smiled. "That's where cost-benefit analysis comes in. When you're deciding whether to buy something, ask yourself, 'Is the benefit worth the cost?' or 'Do I need this?' and 'Is that new video game worth the money you could save for a car?"

Trey contemplated this. "Maybe not," he admitted. "I could save that money for the car instead."

Destiny agreed, "And I think I need to cut back on clothes and eating out, and I need to start putting more towards my college savings."

After Destiny and Trey completed their budget, which included their income and expenses, they realized how much money they had left.

Mom helped them calculate how much they could realistically save each month based on their income and expenses. Over the next few weeks, they worked to adjust their habits.

Destiny discovered the joys of cooking at home instead of eating out. She also found creative ways to mix and match her style by switching up her outfit choices. She even discovered the value of thrift stores as an alternative to buying brand-new clothes.

Trey learned to prioritize his car fund over the latest video games. He even found ways to earn extra income by selling his unwanted video games.

Destiny and Trey watched their savings accounts grow steadily as the weeks passed. The initial anxiety about budgeting had transformed into a sense of accomplishment and control over their finances.

They gathered with their mom every week to review their progress and adjust their plans as needed. Mom instilled in them the importance of delayed gratification, conducting a cost-benefit analysis, and the power of compound interest as they saved.

They even started planning for future expenses, like car insurance and college dorm costs.

Trey discovered that owning a car was not just about the initial purchase but would also involve maintenance and gas expenses. He researched the cost of regular oil changes, tire replacements, and gas prices in their area to estimate a realistic monthly budget for his car.

On the other hand, Destiny learned about the importance of academic achievements in securing funds for her college education. She found that many scholarships and grants are available for students who demonstrate exceptional academic performance and that maintaining good grades can increase her eligibility for financial aid.

She researched various scholarships and grants and began exploring the application process for each one.

Over time, budgeting became a habit, a valuable tool they used to navigate the often tricky financial terrain of teenage life.

They became more responsible, prioritizing their goals and making informed decisions about their money.

One evening, as Destiny balanced her budget book with a satisfied smile, she looked up at her mom and said, "Thank you, Mom. You've taught us so much more than just budgeting. You've empowered us to take charge of our future." Trey nodded in agreement, adding, "We finally understand the value of money and the importance of making smart choices. We'll never forget this."

Mom's heart swelled with pride. Her children were not just learning about money; they were learning valuable life lessons about responsibility, discipline, and planning for the future. As she looked at their determined faces, she smiled and said, "Saving for the future is important, but it's equally important to enjoy life today," Mom reminded them. "The key is to find a balance between saving and spending."

Trey eventually purchased his dream car, a used but reliable model he purchased with his meticulously saved funds.

He always ensured he had enough money for car maintenance and insurance expenses.

Destiny, equipped with a solid financial plan, embarked on her academic journey at her dream college, confident in her ability to manage her finances and achieve her goals.

With the help of college scholarships, she was able to fund her college education, and the money she saved would be used for her other expenses.

Throughout their journey, their mom's guidance and encouragement were invaluable. She wasn't just teaching them about budgeting; she was teaching them valuable life lessons about responsibility, discipline, and the power of taking control of their financial future. And as they embarked on their individual paths, they knew they were equipped with the tools and knowledge to navigate the financial world with confidence and success.

Definitions and Examples

Budgeting: Planning how to spend your money over a specific period, like a month or a year.

> **Example:** You track your income (money earned) and expenses (money spent) to make sure you don't spend more than you earn. This helps you reach your financial goals, like buying a car or saving for college.

Cost/Benefit Analysis: Weighing the pros and cons of a decision, especially considering the cost (money spent) and the benefit (value or enjoyment gained).

> **Example:** You're deciding whether to buy a new video game. You consider the cost of the game, your existing games, and how much time you have to play. You might decide the benefit of having fun outweighs the cost.

Compound Interest: Earning interest on your interest. It makes your money grow over time as it's saved in a savings account.

> **Example:** If you save $100 in a savings account with a 2% interest rate, you will earn $2 in interest after one month, which means you'll have $102 in your account. In the second month, you will earn interest on the new balance of $102, earning $2.04, and your account balance will grow to $104.04. As time passes, your interest will increase and your savings will grow.

Fixed Expenses: Costs that stay the same each month, like rent, phone bill, or car insurance.

> **Example:** You pay $500 each month for rent. This is a fixed expense because the amount doesn't change.

Variable Expenses: Costs that change each month, like groceries, gas, or entertainment.

> **Example:** You spend $100 on groceries one week and $75 the next week. This is a variable expense because the amount changes.

PERSONAL SPENDING TRACKER

WEEK OF:

DATE	DESCRIPTION	AMOUNT	CASH/CARD

CREATE YOUR OWN BUDGET

INCOME

Income 1		
Income 2		
Others		
	Total Income:	

EXPENSES

Month

Budget

BILLS TO BE PAID	DUE DATE	AMOUNT	PAID	NOTE
	TOTAL			

MONTHLY SUMMARY

TOTAL INCOME	TOTAL EXPENSES	DIFFERENCES

NOTES

ABOUT THE AUTHOR

Annette Harris is a wife, mother, and avid volunteer in her community. She is a military veteran who spent eight years in the United States Army with two wartime deployments (Afghanistan and Iraq). She has earned nine degrees, three Masters, three Bachelors, and three Associates, from 2003 to 2021. She graduated from Florida State University, Webster University, Liberty University, and Columbia College of Missouri.

She is a certified human resources professional with over 15 years in the field. Annette is an online Adjunct Professor in Human Resources Management. She also owns Harris Financial Coaching and is a certified Financial Fitness Coach (FFC) and Accredited Financial Counselor.

As a teenager, Annette was inspired by her mother to learn more about managing money. She has since passed on that same passion for financial literacy to her children, with Destiny, the youngest, providing daily inspiration. Annette is now on a mission to empower young girls and women to achieve financial freedom by educating them on money management.

More From the Mommy, Can You Teach Me Series

Book 1: Mommy, Can You Teach Me About Money?

Book 2: Mommy, Can You Teach Me How To Save?

Book 2.5: Mommy, Can You Teach Me How to Budget?

Book 3: Mommy, Can You Teach Me How To Invest?

www.ingramcontent.com/pod-product-compliance
Lightning Source LLC
LaVergne TN
LVHW070901210926
848482LV00016D/987
* 9 7 9 8 9 8 8 4 0 7 3 4 8 *